# 1001 WAYS TO
# HAPPINESS

*With special thanks to Anne Moreland*

**ARCTURUS**

This edition published in 2013 by Arcturus Publishing Limited
26/27 Bickels Yard, 151–153 Bermondsey Street,
London SE1 3HA

ISBN: 978-1-84858-545-4
AD002187EN

Printed in China

# **Contents**

# Introduction

Since ancient times, religious thinkers, philosophers, writers, and artists have reflected on how to achieve the balanced state of happiness and contentment that we all, as human beings, seek to attain. In this little book, we look at some of the way

they have suggested, adding the thoughts of many unknown individuals who have nonetheless contributed to our store of knowledge on this essential subject. Some of this advice is serious, some light-hearted; some profound, some funny. Together, the gems of wisdom you will find in these pages make up a guide to that most contradictory and elusive of human goals: happiness.

# What is
# Happiness?

How do we define happiness? Is it a state that we all agree on, or does it vary from culture to culture, and from individual to individual?

When we approve of ourselves, rather than always seeking approval from others, we find happiness.

# When one door closes, another opens.

The path to happiness is paved with dreams, but don't forget to admire the beauty of the landscape as you travel.

**Make your own happiness; it's up to you.**

Don't spend your life looking back; remember the good times, but look forward to new ones.

# If you make someone else happy, you make yourself happy.

*Carpe diem* –
seize the day.

People in difficult circumstances can be happy, while those who live a life of ease may be miserable.

Don't expect answers; rather, ask, what's the question?

Be curious about the world around you;
try to learn as much as you can about it.

# If you're unhappy, don't try to hide it. Express it, then let it go.

**Love can turn sorrow into happiness.**

To be happy, you need to know that others love you for yourself, just as you are.

Human beings adapt quickly to pleasure, which means we tend not to value the ordinary.

# Solitude may bring happiness.

# If you fear losing your happiness, you must have some happiness to lose.

Let go of sadness. Don't allow it to become a comfort zone.

**It is better to travel than to arrive.**

Happiness is meeting an old friend you haven't seen for years, and picking up where you left off.

**Sometimes happiness is free; sometimes, it comes at a cost.**

Everyone has a different idea of happiness. Follow your own path, not someone else's.

# We often make ourselves unhappy by wanting contradictory things in life.

## **Joy and sorrow come hand in hand.**

Don't feel guilty if the things that are supposed to make you happy fail to do so.

Having achieved a special goal in life can make you happy, but there may also be a feeling of anti-climax – before you begin to aim for a new one.

# Life is full of care, but there are always moments of joy along the way.

My motto is: contented with little, wishing for more.

*Charles Lamb*

Happiness: a calm awareness of the present moment, of sensation, consciousness, thoughts, and perception.

# Laughter is the best medicine.

The glass is half full
for some people,
half empty for others.
Becoming happy
may simply involve a
change of perspective.

**A loving family and friends
... that's happiness.**

We all dream of that cottage in the country with roses round the door, but wouldn't life be dull if all our dreams were fulfilled?

# Be happy you're alive!

# When you make a cup of tea, don't hurry. Savour the process.

No one can be unhappy all the time, just as no one can be happy all the time.

# Nature surviving in glorious simplicity makes us happy.

The person who lives in their own home, eats and lives simply, and has no debt to anyone, is truly happy.

There is no way to happiness; happiness is the way.

**Sleeping soundly, and waking refreshed, is one of life's blessings.**

# Never forget the magic you believed in as a child.

**It is not the position in which you stand, but the direction in which you look.**

You can't expect to be happy all the time. Human beings are not made that way.

# A good, long soak in a hot bath will wash your cares away.

# Make happiness your goal, and do whatever it takes to achieve it.

Don't try to define what happiness is; instead, think about what makes you unhappy, and try to change it.

# Happiness is a warm puppy.

Nurturing and loving someone is the key to happiness.

**Be a little crazy now and then. Life is far too serious, so when you can, be a child again.**

**Once our basic needs are satisfied, our level of wealth has no effect on how happy we are.**

If everyone gets richer, no one feels better off.

Those who are valued by their community are often happier than those who achieve public success.

# Listen to the purr of a cat: that's the sound of happiness.

# Happiness grows when you notice it.

People travel far and wide looking for happiness. Sometimes, when they come back home, they find it waiting for them on the doorstep.

# Take time to be sad ... and then move on.

Loving relationships are the most important factor in happiness. Next comes work, and the meaning it can bring.

You're a long time dead, so be happy in the short time you have to live.

# Travel along the road of love, for at the end of the road lies happiness.

A good deed can benefit you as much as it does the other person.

Contentment is a pearl of great price, and whoever procures it at the expense of ten thousand desires makes a wise and a happy purchase. *John Balguy*

# The sweetest moments are the shortest.

Slow down and enjoy life.
Otherwise you may forget
where you're going, and why.

**The smallest things in life bring happiness
– watch a flower grow, or a bird fly by.**

# Happiness is contagious.

A person who is contented with what he has done will never become famous for what he will do.

Happiness has magical properties. It leads to long life, health, and resilience.

# Contentment is natural wealth, luxury is artificial poverty. *Socrates*

Watching a bee take nectar from a flower you've grown is a happy sight to see.

Like harmony in music, happiness is when every part of yourself comes together in agreement.

# There is no happiness without dreams.

# Being miserable involves certainty; being happy involves risk.

The story of wealth failing to translate into happiness is the story of the Western world.

# Joy is a flower that blooms when you do.

Good humour is one of the best articles of dress one can wear in society. *William Thackeray*

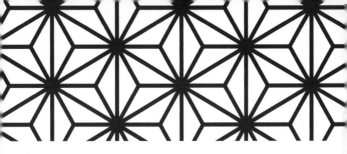

Contentment is being satisfied with things as they are, not as you would like them to be.

Feel, show, and express your happiness, so that others can share it, too.

# Even in a happy life, there are moments of despair.

If we have not quiet in our minds, outward comfort will do no more for us than a golden slipper on a gouty foot. *John Bunyan*

Happiness, the thing we want most in life, is often achieved by giving it away.

**To be content, we need to experience a sense of meaning, and a sense of achievement.**

# Happiness is a natural outcome of being able to be oneself.

There is a connection between being grateful and being happy. But who knows which one leads to the other?

# Happiness is a full belly.

Activities that involve us in the natural world – whether feeding the birds, stroking the cat, or going for a country walk – help us to feel happier.

Happiness is a decision, involving choice, action, and faith.

Don't envy other people's happiness – what makes them happy might not have the same effect on you.

# Whenever you feel creative, playful, or silly, you are close to being happy.

# Happiness is a state of mind that is open, friendly, and positive.

**The original meaning of the word 'happiness' is 'good fortune,' or 'luck'.**

Gardens are the places we make to be happy in ...
with a little help from nature.

# Happiness is the emotional aspect of health.

Looking at a great work of art can bring a sense of beauty, order, peace, and contentment.

# Being happy is known to boost the immune system.

Our happiness is threatened whenever we act in a way that is not true to ourselves.

# In order to be happy, we must first know sadness.

# Happiness is the absence of fear.

**Achieving your goals is success; enjoying what you've achieved is happiness.**

# Sing when you're happy – whatever you sound like!

Anticipation of a happy event can make you happier than the event itself.

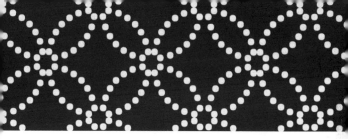

Happiness is running outside after the first snowfall of winter, throwing snowballs, and making a snowman.

# Remembered happiness is the most perfect.

**A flower in bloom …
a cloudless sky …
a child's laughter –
these are the gifts that
can make us happy, if
we choose to let them.**

Happiness is eating a peach,
warmed by the sun.

Happiness is good for you. It produces endorphins, natural chemicals that act as painkillers.

# Creativity is a catalyst for happiness.

People who touch and
are receptive to touch are
more likely to be happy.

**Regular exercise boosts happiness, especially when performed with others.**

A dog is a great comfort when you're feeling unhappy, because it never asks why.

# We may pass violets looking for roses.

Learn to be pleased with everything; with wealth, so far as it makes us beneficial to others; with poverty, for not having much to care for; and with obscurity, for being unenvied. *Plutarch*

# Tears of joy are the sweetest tears of all.

**What makes us unhappy with ourselves is the exaggerated idea we have of the happiness of others.**

Gather ye rosebuds
while ye may
Old time is still a-flying
And this same flower
that smiles today
Tomorrow will be dying.

*Robert Herrick*

# Finding the Way

How can we begin to find contentment? Let's look at the many different steps we can take towards making happiness our goal.

# Heal yourself with happy thoughts.

Don't tell unhappy people how happy you are. Instead, use your happiness to help them …

**You can find happiness in many different places. In the colours of a painting … in the clouds above your head … the earth under your feet … in the rosy pink sky of dawn … and the pure white snow of winter …**

It is right to be contented with what we have, but never with what we are.
*James Mackintosh*

# Don't refuse to accept the gift of happiness, just because you are afraid of losing it.

Coming home to your dog is one of the most joyous events of the day – both for you, and for your dog!

# Happiness is a gift that cannot be bought.

Pay attention to the thoughts that drift across your mind. Some of them may be important.

**Do not spoil what you have by desiring what you have not; remember that what you now have was once among the things you only hoped for.** *Epicurus*

If you approach work with passion and energy, it will help you to be happy.

# Happiness is an adventure. Set out on it.

There are many roads to pleasure, but only one true path to happiness.

**Content makes poor men rich; discontentment makes rich men poor.** *Benjamin Franklin*

**Happiness is curling up with a good book beside a crackling fire on a cold winter's night**

Be content with your lot; one cannot be first in everything.
*Aesop*

## Since we cannot always get what we like, let us like what we can get.

Some see darkness, misery, and despair in a rainy day: others, a sacred blessing from the heavens, refreshing us and giving life to all plants and creatures on this earth.

# Swimming in clear, warm, blue seawater is one of life's joys.

**Creative people are often unhappy. If they weren't, they wouldn't bother to be creative.**

## Happiness is like a fruit – don't eat it until it is ripe!

Unhappiness is not all bad – it can lead to struggle, and struggle can lead to change.

# A little bit of what you fancy does you good.

Sometimes we lose the key to happiness, not realizing that the door is always unlocked.

**Moderation in all things.**

**If we human beings had tails to wag when we're happy, like dogs, we might understand each other better.**

When we're happy, we often don't know it. When we're unhappy, we always do.

If you have to ask what happiness is, you'll never know.

**A brief moment of happiness can lighten even the darkest despair.**

Take a good long laugh at yourself … it may help to make you happy.

# Be your own best friend.

Don't search for happiness itself. Instead, concentrate on the activities that make you feel happy.

# Happiness can see you. Can you see it?

Happy the man, and happy he alone, he who can call today his own; he who, secure within, can say, tomorrow do thy worst, for I have lived today. *John Dryden*

To be happy in life, it helps if you don't think too much.

**Happiness can make an ordinary sight beautiful.**

**The key to happiness is patience.**

When you can think of yesterday without regret, and tomorrow without fear, then you are near to happiness.

The colder the water in the pool, the warmer your glow when you've had your swim.

Follow your own advice before dispensing it to others.

**A hearty meal, and good company to share it with, is the perfect end to a happy day.**

Happiness is not the fulfilment of what you want, but the realization of how much you already have.

# A rich man is one who has no need of wealth.

**Be yourself, with all your faults and strengths.**

Don't let little things get you down. Keep a sense of perspective.

**You will only fail if you stop trying.**

It is important to feel valued. Stay close to those who value you, and distance yourself from those who do not.

# In the war against fear, joy is the best weapon.

There are short cuts to happiness, and dancing is one of them. *Vicki Baum*

**Conquer your fears by facing them. If you retreat, they will loom larger in your life.**

# You are a force of nature to be reckoned with.

If at first you don't succeed, you are just like everyone else. It's called learning.

**Everyone deserves to be happy. It is within your power to become so.**

Friendship is a cornerstone of happiness.

You can dance anywhere, if only in your heart.

**If you are a thoughtful, kind friend, you will be happier … whether or not your friends return the compliment.**

When you tend your garden, you also tend your soul.

Do not argue with the inevitable.

**Happiness is about having the right frame of mind, not the right circumstances.**

# Be careful what you wish for.

Trust yourself. Then you will know how to live.

# Forgive your enemies – it will really annoy them!

Energy spent worrying is mostly wasted energy.

Stand fast, like a tree … your roots deep in the soil … unshakeable in the wind and rain …

**A long walk in the countryside, in the company of a good friend, is one of life's greatest joys.**

Sometimes we sail into troubled waters, but if we are patient, in time, we will sail out again.

Try to get through a day without wanting or not wanting.

# In the hustle and bustle of life, find a quiet place … inside your mind.

Become absorbed in your activities, so that you are at one with what you are doing.

Don't wake up at night and worry. Wait until morning, when you'll find the problem has got smaller!

**Solitude can be a friend and guide, leading you to happiness.**

# Learn to spend time with yourself.

Bringing love, luck, and happiness into your life takes hard work. It doesn't happen by itself.

# Kindness costs nothing, and can bring so much happiness.

# Admiration is possible without envy.

Everything flows and nothing abides.

*Heraclitus*

Don't resist change – if you do, you will turn happiness to sorrow.

**Concentrate on the task in hand. However trivial, you will feel happier if you do it well.**

Run as fast as you can,
and no faster.

**Honesty has
the power to
destroy fear.**

If you want happiness for an hour – take a nap. If you want happiness for a day – go fishing. If you want happiness for a lifetime – help someone else.

*Chinese proverb*

# Happiness opens the arms and closes the eyes.

**Happiness is like a perfume. You cannot pour it on others without getting a few drops on yourself.**

# Only moments of happiness stay with us.

A merchant's happiness hangs upon chance, wind, and waves.
*Japanese proverb*

# Sleep soundly and happiness may visit you in your dreams.

A day well lived makes yesterday a dream of happiness and tomorrow a vision of hope. *Indian proverb*

**Exercising the body brings rest to the mind.**

The creative play of the imagination is essential to human happiness.

**Pray for a healthy mind in a healthy body.**
*Juvenal*

To boost happiness, watch young children play – and join in the fun, if you can!

# At the peak of happiness, we stop thinking. Instead, we find peace.

Make sure you do something you enjoy every day; however busy you are, find time to fit it in…

**Never impose on others what you would not choose for yourself.** *Confucius*

A walk, run, or any kind of exercise in the fresh air will help to brighten your day.

**Dance first. Think later. It's the natural order.**

*Samuel Beckett*

**Cut down on multi-tasking. It tires the mind, and achieves little of value.**

Give someone a 'gratitude gift'. Write down all the reasons you are grateful to them, and tell them.

# It is a wise man who knows the extent of his ignorance.

Creativity is not something mystical – it's something you already know.

Do not go where the path may lead, go instead where there is no path and leave a trail.
*Ralph Waldo Emerson*

**Valuing others, and being valued, as part of a family, community, or enterprise, is a certain path to happiness.**

**Concentration helps to relax the mind.**

Make a list of things that make you happy. You'll find there are more of them than you imagined...

# Can you draw how it feels to be happy?

Take time to sit down and listen to a piece of music without doing anything else.

**Anyone who says sunshine brings happiness has never danced in the rain.**

# The world is but a canvas to the imagination.

*Henry David Thoreau*

The art of happiness is like any other – the more you practise it, the better you get at it.

**Happy people don't have the best of everything; they make the best of everything.**

Happy are the painters, for they shall not be lonely. Light and colour, peace and hope, shall keep them to the end of the day.

*Winston Churchill*

# Creativity is within everyone's reach – no exceptions. And to be creative, even in a small way, can bring great happiness.

Capture your daydreams. Keep them safely, and think of them often.

Criticism always cuts deep into our hearts. Praise often makes no impression at all. Learn to listen to the praise, as well as the blame.

**Build a happiness habit. List five things per day that have made you happy.**

There is a crucial link between happiness and altruism, or 'regard for others'.

**To have his path made clear for him is the aspiration of every human being in our beclouded and tempestuous existence.** *Joseph Conrad*

# People who exercise their brains stay young in spirit.

**Identify the strengths you have developed through the years, and work out how you can harness them in solving your problems.**

Try to notice when you're happy.

**If you respect yourself, you will not be so upset when others show disrespect for you.**

**When you feel overwhelmed by life's challenges, look back at the past and remember difficult times you've survived.**

March on. Do not tarry. To go forward is to move toward perfection. March on, and fear not the thorns, or the sharp stones on life's path. *Khalil Gibran*

# A kind heart and an open mind are the best travelling companions.

Feed your soul – meditate, walk by the sea, listen to music, visit art galleries and historic buildings. If you do, you'll feel more balanced.

**Try to see the best in people.**

The front left side of the brain is the part that registers happiness, wellbeing, and contentment. Make sure to exercise it!

Travel in hope, but live in happiness.

Simple meditation can boost happiness. Every day, find a few minutes to sit somewhere quiet. Close your eyes, breathe slowly, and just watch your thoughts come and go.

# Believing you're a good person is easier if you act like one.

**Travel broadens the mind ... and lifts the soul.**

# Activity

The Greek philosopher Aristotle saw happiness as 'human flourishing', or 'working towards virtue'. Is happiness achieved through selfless dedication, work, or in other ways?

Filter out your toxic language. Don't run yourself down, even to be funny. When you talk in negatives, you build a negative mindset.

**Work connects us to others, building a happier world for everyone.**

To find out what one is fitted to do, and to secure an opportunity to do it, is the key to happiness. *John Dewey*

# Speak less, listen more.

# Human beings are hard-wired for love and compassion.

Ask yourself, what are you grateful for? You'll find many answers.

**Five keys to happier living: giving; relating; appreciating; accepting; questing.**

**Show affection, say thank you, and express what you value in friends, family, and workmates.**

We cannot do great things on this earth – only small things with great love.
*Mother Teresa*

# Work expands to fill the time available.

Crank up the sunny side of your brain by spending time in the zone known as 'flow'. This is when you're so absorbed in a pleasurable activity that you tune out of everything else.

Any activity becomes creative when the doer cares about doing it right or better.
*John Updike*

# Opportunities for kindness pop up all over the place – look out for them!

**Fear closes down our minds and our hearts.**

Constant criticism is highly destructive in relationships. For every negative comment, find five positive ones to add.

All growth depends upon activity.
There is no development physically
or intellectually without effort, and
effort means work. *Calvin Coolidge*

# Be present
# in all you do.

Each day, notice an object of wonder or beauty. Take a moment to appreciate the skill that went into creating it.

## He who hesitates is lost.

When you're doing something you enjoy, savour it: the warm water when you take a shower, a moment of calm at the end of the day.

# Life grants nothing to us mortals without hard work.
*Horace*

It is rare to find a selfish person who is truly happy.

Eat slowly. Notice the colours, textures, and flavours, of your food, how it feels in your mouth. That way, you'll really enjoy it … and you won't stuff yourself!

**Compliment someone whose behaviour has impressed you, even if you feel shy about doing so. Most people will appreciate it.**

Lack of activity destroys the good condition of every human being, while movement and methodical physical exercise save it and preserve it. *Plato*

**Finding new avenues for your talents in new ways increases happiness – your own, and that of others.**

**We are most true to ourselves when we're about nine or ten. So revisit that time in your life by taking up the hobbies that you enjoyed as a child.**

Identify your strengths and weaknesses as a person. Then work on the strengths!

Action is the highest perfection and drawing forth of the utmost power, vigour, and activity of man's nature.
*Bishop Robert South*

**Build some variation into your life. Take a different route to work, try food from a different culture, or visit a museum or gallery you've never been to before.**

# Actions speak louder than words.

Research shows that the happiness of a close contact increases the chance of being happy by fifteen per cent.

Happiness fuels success, not the other way round.

**When we're positive, we become more motivated, engaged, energetic, resilient, and productive.**

The only exercise some people get is jumping to conclusions, running down their friends, side-stepping responsibility, and pushing their luck ...

**Go confidently in your dreams. Live the life you have imagined.** *Henry David Thoreau*

Our genetic make-up is thought to influence about fifty per cent of the variation in our personal happiness. The rest is up to us!

**Giving money away makes people feel happier than spending it on themselves.**

**Parents usually wish, first and foremost, for their children to be happy. That's quite an ambition for a child to live up to …**

Identify irrational and unhelpful thoughts, and learn to deal with them.

The harder I work, the luckier I get.
*Samuel Goldwyn*

**Half an hour's meditation each day is essential, except when you are busy. Then a full hour is needed.**

*St Francis de Sales*

Reach out to help a friend in need – you can help them to see light at the end of the tunnel.

# The journey is the reward.

**Compassion is at the heart of happiness.**

Make time to bring a friend flowers or a plant; to bake them a cake; or to send them an amusing link, or funny photo.

If you're feeling sad, don't pretend to be happy. Be yourself, and the mood will pass.

# Well begun is half done. *Aristotle*

# Set goals, big or small. Write them down. Be specific, rather than general.

**The journey of a thousand miles starts with a single step.** *Chinese proverb*

Don't expect to be a perfect parent – acknowledge your mistakes, and move on.

You've got to find what you love and that is as true for work as it is for lovers … If you haven't found it yet, keep looking and don't settle. As with all matters of the heart, you'll know when you've found it. *Steve Jobs*

**Celebrate success; take time to enjoy it, and thank those who helped you get there.**

To everything there is a season, and a time to every purpose under heaven.
*Ecclesiastes*

Ten minutes of meditation per day can help us be happier, more optimistic, and more spiritually aware.

It is not always events that cause a reaction, but our negative responses to them, which we can sometimes control.

# No one can stop the march of time.

**A bear, however hard he tries Grows tubby without exercise.**

*A. A. Milne*

The way we interpret life events has a bearing on our happiness.

If you feel jealous of others, take a closer look at their lives, and ask, would I really want to be them?

**Better to light a candle than curse the darkness.**

Tune in to your negative, irrational, or unhelpful thoughts, and challenge them.

If we can first find our true purpose, and then pursue it, we may find happiness.

**Derive happiness in oneself from a good day's work, from illuminating the fog that surrounds us.**

*Henri Matisse*

At the heart of a happy
relationship is good
communication.

**Challenge all thoughts that begin, 'What if …?'**

Recognize your needs and the needs of others – that way you won't become tangled up in misunderstandings.

**Beware of 'black and white thinking'. Ask yourself what is the worst that could happen, what is the best, and what is the most likely.**

# Commit to be fit.

Your work is to discover your work and then with all your heart to give yourself to it. *Buddha*

If we worry a lot, we get into bad mental habits. Rationalizing our fears is one way to banish them.

**Failing to plan is planning to fail.**

*Alan Lakein*

People who have a vocation in life tend to be happier.

**Sharing our thoughts and needs makes us feel valued and understood.**

# Practice makes perfect.

We all share these common needs: to belong, to experience joy, to feel safe, and to be treated with respect.

**If your dog is fat, you're not getting enough exercise.**

**Other people can trigger our emotions, but the choice is ours about how we respond.**

# Don't put off till tomorrow what you could do today. After all, there's no time like the present.

Work is love made visible. And if you cannot work with love but only with distaste, it is better that you should leave your work and sit at the gate of the temple and take alms of those who work with joy.
*Khalil Gibran*

A simple 'hello' to a neighbour can make us feel happier and more secure about where we live.

# The shoemaker's son often goes barefoot.

*English proverb*

There is hope, even in the most difficult circumstances.

**If someone wants to share good news with you, ask questions, listen, smile, and help them relive the experience.**

Genius is one per cent inspiration, ninety-nine per cent perspiration.
**Thomas Edison**

Giving support and receiving it from others helps us to be happy.

**Think about how and when you experience feelings of happiness in your life. It's different for everyone.**

**Success has many fathers, while failure is an orphan.**

Be genuinely pleased for others when things go well for them. It's not as hard as you think.

# Honesty is the best policy.

Ask yourself what the meaning and purpose of your life is. You may not discover the answer, but it will help you to focus on what matters to you.

# Work, rest, and play… the balance in life can be hard to keep, but it is possible.

**Break the loop of negative thinking.**

Try not to look at the clock too much. Remember, a watched pot never boils …

**If you make a mistake, don't keep going over it. Acknowledge it, try to make amends, and then forget about it.**

**A little knowledge is a dangerous thing.**

Don't be intimidated by the task ahead. Mighty oaks from little acorns grow!

**Write down everything that matters to you, and then list them in priority. It will help you focus on the important things in life.**

Doing nothing is very hard to do … you never know when you're finished.

# A change is as good as a rest.

Don't compare yourselves negatively to other people. They may be having problems in their personal life that you don't know about.

**Fun is a serious business.**

Detox your negative thoughts. It takes willpower and determination, but you can do it!

**If you feel overworked, try to take a break. Get outdoors, and blow the cobwebs away…**

# Identify the situations, places, and people that make you unhappy. Then avoid them.

If wishes were horses, beggars would ride.

Try to come to terms with the fact that you can't have everything in life. It's obvious, but it's something we often forget!

**Be a realistic optimist – have a positive outlook, but be aware of the constraints in your life.**

# Early to bed and early to rise, makes a man healthy, wealthy, and wise.

'Reframe' events: try to see the best, not the worst, in what happened.

**The only place success comes before work is in the dictionary.**
*Vince Lombardi*

Be open to opportunity.

# There is no happiness without struggle.

Never ignore your dreams for the future – they will help to guide you on your way.

**What's the gap between how you want to live and how you do live? Can you close it? Describe in detail your vision of the future for yourself – then work towards it.**

All work and no play makes Jack a dull boy.

Imagine yourself ten years from now. What would you like to happen? Set goals, and you may find you can realize them!

# Nobody notices what we do, until we stop doing it…

# When things go wrong, don't always blame yourself.

Don't pressure yourself to be happy. Instead, create a positive mindset: be open, appreciate, curious, and kind.

Let go of rigid expectations and expand awareness of natural beauty and human kindness.

# All things are difficult before they are easy.

*Thomas Fuller*

# Think in terms of 'we', not in terms of 'me'.

Our emotions give flavour to our lives.

Make a list of your ten most positive emotions. Joy, pride, gratitude, inspiration … you choose.

**Because I have work to care about, it is possible that I may be less difficult to get along with than other women when the double chins start to form.**
*Gloria Steinem*

**Don't give yourself a hard time –
self-acceptance is the key to wellbeing**

# A good beginning makes a good ending.

There's no such thing as a free lunch.

**Hard work spotlights the character of people: some turn up their sleeves, some turn up their noses, and some don't turn up at all.**
*Sam Ewing*

# A State of Being

In modern times, happiness is seen as a private emotional state, achieved through self-fulfilment. Is spiritual enlightenment, rather than activity, the way to happiness? Or is it, perhaps, a combination of both?

**Don't ask 'Why'? Instead, ask 'Why not'**

When we are young, we think we know everything. In old age, we find out we know nothing.

**If one man kills a hundred men, and another masters himself, the second is the greater warrior.**
*Buddha*

**Kindness to others boosts happiness. It increases life satisfaction, provides a sense of meaning, and takes our minds off our own troubles.**

# A single moment of happiness can rub out hours of misery.

Turn the rocks in your path into stepping stones to help you along your way.

When you wake up in the morning, pause for a moment to honour the gift of another day.

The journey is the destination.

There are no rewards and punishments in life; only consequences.

**What matters most in parenting is not strict routine, but providing unconditional love for children and helping them to feel understood, valued, and secure.**

If the sight of a blue sky fills you with joy, be happy, for your soul is alive.

Remember, you don't have to have an opinion on everything.

**What goes around comes around –
and with kindness, it really does.**

Acknowledge your
mistakes as soon
as you make them
… before others
point them out.

# Live for today – tomorrow may never come.

People pay for what they do, and still more for what they have allowed themselves to become. And they pay for it very simply; by the lives they lead. *James Baldwin*

# Life is a journey to an unknown destination, from which the traveller never returns

Don't be afraid to travel. Go, and when you come back, you will find you are a braver person.

Generosity is not just about money – we can also give time, ideas, and energy.

**Think of unhappiness as a job you've walked out on.**

Don't let obstacles in life stand in your way. If you can't jump over them, go round them.

# Success is never a measure of happiness.

# Don't go looking for opportunities – instead, make them happen.

To fail in business is misfortune, but to fail in life is tragic.

A cynic is a man who knows the price of everything and the value of nothing. *Oscar Wilde*

As you travel, don't forget to stop sometimes and admire the view.

**The optimist turns problems into opportunities. The pessimist does the reverse.**

**You will only envy others if you have a low opinion of yourself.**

Don't be too quick to criticize others. Let them make their own mistakes

# Virtue is its own reward.

All joy in this world comes from wanting others to be happy, and all the suffering from wanting only oneself to be happy.

Try to be polite in all situations, however annoying you find people – you will feel better for it.

**Giving to others can be a simple kind word, or gesture.**

**Travel in your mind, as well as your body.**

Your best may not be enough, but if you give of it, you will have no regrets.

**Practise random acts of kindness.**

Fear less, hope more
Whine less, breathe more
Talk less, say more
Hate less, love more
And all good things
are yours. *Swedish proverb*

If you never travel, you may be hiding from the adventure of the open road; if you make the open road your home, you may be hiding from the commitment of domestic life.

Treat each person you meet with respect – appearances may be deceptive.

# Your actions are your only true possessions.

Meditation can lead to structural brain changes thought to be associated with happiness.

In the city, we long for the peace and quiet of the countryside; in the country, we miss the bright lights.

**Learn to accept your thoughts, rather than trying to control them.**

Some people walk in the rain.
Others just get wet.
*Roger Miller*

# It takes commitment and determination to be happy.

**Frame your photos and diplomas. Personal objects are not just décor, they're psychological supports, increasing our sense of self and achievement.**

When we return home after a trip, we often see our normal way of life with new eyes, and can truly appreciate the blessings we have. In this way, we learn about our lives through change.

# Gratitude is good for us. It increases positive emotion and decreases the negative.

Mindfulness is a state of open, active attention on the present. It means living in the moment and awakening to experience.

Observe your thoughts from a distance, without judging them to be good or bad.

**An individual who stays in the same place all his life may find as much to interest him as a person who travels the whole world.**

Suffering is caused by craving. Stop craving, and your suffering will cease.

**When someone is talking to you, instead of thinking your own thoughts, listen to what they have to say.**

Make time for people that need help, regardless of whether they are friends or not.

**Research shows that minimalist interiors can be depressing. So paint your walls bright colours; it will help to lift your mood.**

Walking through a dark forest, one is sometimes afraid – perhaps not of what may lurk among the trees, but of listening to oneself in the stillness.

Keep connected to your fellow human being and to nature.

**The path to happiness can be steep, difficult and stony, while the path to misery can be downhill all the way.**

Do not meet anger with anger. Count to ten, and ask yourself, why is this person so angry? If you pay attention, you may find out.

# Respect is a form of love.

# Don't let life pass you by. Live in the present, savouring each moment.

Acknowledge that you are special – there's no one quite like you.

# The Cycle of Life

Being able to embrace the present, without worrying about the past and the future, is cruicial to being happy. But having an overview of the process of our entire lives is also necessary.

# The sound of happiness is a running stream.

The paradox of life is that as we grow older in our bodies, we grow younger in our minds, reliving the days of our childhood with a new intensity.

**To be idle is a short road to death and to be diligent is a way of life; foolish people are idle, wise people are diligent.**

*Buddha*

The mystery of how time passes by so quickly, and yet so slowly, is one that human beings will never understand.

Life is short, so don't waste a second of it!

# Happiness is the greatest gift a person can have or bestow.

**A sorrow shared is a sorrow halved**

To dwell on unhappiness is a waste of time. And wasting time is wasting life.

# Live as if today might be your last.

When someone dies, at the exact same moment, a new person comes into the world. Thus the eternal cycle of life continues.

Do not base your happiness on material wealth. It can disappear all too quickly.

Life is not just a journey to the grave. It's an adventure to be set out on with courage and optimism.

Force of habit, or routine, can blind us to the wonders of the world around us.

Life is a jest, and all things show it
I thought so once, and now I know it.
*John Gay*

**Don't envy another's happiness;
instead, try to share in it.**

# If you accept yourself as you are, you may find others follow suit

**It is possible to provide security against other ills, but as far as death is concerned, we men live in a city without walls.** *Epicurus*

Watching the sun come up in the morning reminds us that all is possible when a new day begins.

People facing death often realize for the first time how much they love life. Think how that feels, and try to value what you have now.

Time passes more quickly if we hurry and scurry through life. Instead, stop for a moment, look around, and enjoy it…

**Do not fear death so much as the inadequate life.** *Bertolt Brecht*

We sometimes put ourselves down so as not to appear boastful to our friends. There's no need to do that. Be modest about your achievements, but proud of them also.

**I shall not die of a cold.
I shall die of having lived.**

*Willa Cather*

Listen to what
children say –
sometimes they
see things more
clearly than adults.

**The happy chatter of children is the sound of life.**

People who live life to its full extent seem to have no fear of death.

**Without forgiveness, life is governed by an endless cycle of resentment and retaliation.**
*Roberto Assagioli*

Autumn is bittersweet, the season when fruit ripens … and winter awaits.

**Grieving takes time. Allow yourself to take that time, in order to heal your loss.**

We live one life, but often hanker after several.

# Life is a riddle that we may not be able to solve before we die.

We are all connected to the great circle of life, as beings who live in the midst of nature, and return to nature.

Babies haven't any hair
Old men's heads are just as bare
Between the cradle and the grave
Lies a haircut and a shave.

*Samuel Hoffenstein*

As we grow older, we remember
our childhoods more vividly – the
intensity, the joys, the sorrows.
Recapture that zest for living and
you will stay young at heart.

# Being unhappy is much easier than being happy.

**We strive for happiness in our lives, and when we find it, we become afraid of losing it.**

Eat, drink, and be merry, for tomorrow we diet!

A person lives on in the minds of those who loved them, and those who benefit from what they achieved when they were alive.

If we live in fear, we only live half a life.

**Life is better than death, I believe, if only because it is less boring, and has fresh peaches in it.** *Alice Walker*

Making time and space for yourself will make you happier, however busy you are.

One of the joys of old age is knowing that you have lived a full, active, and happy life. Make sure you come to experience that joy!

**It is easy to see how happy other people are, but we sometimes have trouble noticing it in ourselves.**

The first half of life consists of the capacity to enjoy without the chance; the last half consists of the chance without the capacity. *Mark Twain*

When death comes, let it find you living your life as you please.

Get your work/life balance right. Make clear boundaries, and stick to them. Otherwise your life will slip by without you noticing.

# Man always dies before he is fully born.

*Erich Fromm*

A child lives in the present. A young person in the future. And an old man or woman in the past.

**You have the right to feel happy, sad, or angry, but not always the right to express those emotions whenever you want.**

# If life seems long, that is because you are not really living

**Death is a very dull, dreary affair, and my advice to you is to have nothing to do with it**
*W. Somerset Maugham*

While I thought I was learning how to live, I was learning how to die.
**Leonardo da Vinci**

Life seems to go by faster as we get older. So we have to find ways to slow it down. For example, by celebrating events, going on holiday, and changing our routines.

**Any man's death diminishes me, because I am involved in mankind. And therefore, never send to know for whom the bell tolls; it tolls for thee.** *John Donne*

A happy life is a blessing, not just to the person who lives it, but to the whole world.

Gravestones mark the places where people are buried. Their children, and their achievements, mark the places where they live on.

**I arise in the morning torn between a desire to improve the world and a desire to enjoy the world. This makes it hard to plan the day.** *E.B. White*

Be young, be foolish … but most of all, be happy.

There is only one difference between a long life and a good dinner: that, in the dinner, the sweets come last. *Robert Louis Stevenson*

# Only love is stronger than death.

# Every man dies. Not every man really lives.

*William Wallace*

The cycle of life is everlasting.
After night comes day … after winter,
spring … and after the rain, the sun …

# The Guides

The great philosophers, from the Greeks to the present day, have all puzzled over the question of how to attain happiness. So have artists, writers and several anonymous voices of history. What can they tell us?

Happiness is the purposeful activity of the soul in accordance with virtue. *Aristotle*

One joy scatters a hundred griefs. **Chinese proverb**

**They must often change, who would be constant in happiness or wisdom.** *Confucius*

# To fill the hour – that is happiness.

*Ralph Waldo Emerson*

It is the greatest happiness of the greatest number that is the measure of right and wrong. **Jeremy Bentham.**

# To enjoy good health, to bring true happiness to one's family, one must first discipline and control one's own mind.

*Buddha*

Try to trust others; even if you are proved wrong, it will help to make you happy.

My advice to you is not to inquire why or whither, but just enjoy your ice cream while it's on your plate – that's my philosophy. *Thornton Wilder*

**Truth is a deep kindness that teaches us to be content in our everyday life and share with other people the same happiness.** *Khalil Gibran*

# Love, love, love. That is the soul of genius.

*Wolfgang Amadeus Mozart*

The small share of happiness attainable by man exists only insofar as he is able to cease to think of himself. *Theodore Reik*

Laugh, and the world laughs with you
Weep, and you weep alone.
For the sad old earth must borrow its mirth
But has trouble enough of its own.
*Ella Wheeler Wilcox*

# To make a man happy, add not to his riches, but take away his desires.

*Epicurus*

The man who makes everything that leads to happiness depend upon himself, and not upon other men, has adopted the very best plan for living happily. **Plato**

**Happiness is when what you think, what you say, and what you do, are in harmony.**
*Mohandas Gandhi*

If we want to be happy, we need to put love first.

**It is neither wealth nor splendour, but tranquillity and occupation which bring one happiness.** *Thomas Jefferson*

Fun I love, but too much fun is of all things the most loathsome. Mirth is better than fun, and happiness is better than mirth. *William Blake*

**Friendship has a stronger effect on happiness than income.**

Even if happiness forgets you a little bit, never completely forget about it. *Jacques Prevert*

**A man who as a physical being is always turned toward the outside, thinking that his happiness lies outside him, finally turns inward and discovers that the source is within him.**

*Søren Kierkegaard*

# If you stop looking for happiness, you may find it.

**The essence of philosophy is that a man should so live that his happiness shall depend as little as possible on external things.**

*Epictetus*

If you want to be happy, be.
**Leo Tolstoy**

The supreme happiness of life is the conviction that we are loved; loved for ourselves, or rather in spite of ourselves. *Victor Hugo*

# If you don't ever wonder whether you are happy, you probably are.

He who has so little knowledge of human nature as to seek happiness by changing anything but his own disposition will waste his life in fruitless efforts.

*Samuel Johnson*

A thing of beauty is a joy forever.
**John Keats**

# The best way to cheer yourself up is to try to cheer somebody else up.

*Mark Twain*

Happiness is neither virtue nor pleasure nor this thing nor that, but simply growth. We are happy when we are growing.
**William Butler Yeats**

# Happiness comes when least expected; and departs just as suddenly.

**To have joy one must share it. Happiness was born a twin.**

*Lord Byron*

True happiness comes from the joy of deeds well done, the zest of creating things new.

*Antoine de Saint-Exupéry*

# Happiness is an activity, not an emotion.

**Happiness is not an ideal of reason, but of imagination.**

*Immanuel Kant*

Action may not bring happiness, but there is no happiness without action.
*Benjamin Disraeli*

Can anything be as elegant as to have few wants, and to serve them oneself?

*Ralph Waldo Emerson*

# The two enemies of human happiness are pain and boredom.

*Arthur Schopenhauer*

The only way to avoid being miserable is not to have enough leisure to wonder whether you are happy or not. **George Bernard Shaw**

**When we recall the past, we usually find that it is the simplest things – not the great occasions – that in retrospect give off the greatest glow of happiness.** *Bob Hope*

# Beauty is the promise of happiness.

*Edmund Burke*

Happiness is a mystery, like religion, and should never be rationalized.
**Gilbert K. Chesterton**

The happiness of a man in this life does not consist in the absence but in the mastery of his passions.

**Alfred Lord Tennyson**

**Man is fond of counting his troubles, but he does not count his joys. If he counted them up as he ought to, he would see that every lot has enough happiness provided for it.**

*Fydor Dostoevsky*

# My crown is called content, A crown that seldom kings enjoy... *William Shakespeare*

Man needs, for his happiness, not only the enjoyment of this or that, but hope and enterprise and change. ***Bertrand Russell***

**True happiness is ... to enjoy the present, without anxious dependence upon the future.**
*Seneca*

Success is not the
key to happiness.
key to happiness.
Happiness is the key
to success. *Herman Cain*

I have learned to seek my happiness by limiting my desires, rather than in attempting to satisfy them.
*John Stuart Mill*

**Happiness cannot be traveled to, owned, earned, worn or consumed. Happiness is the spiritual experience of living every minute with love, grace, and gratitude.** *Denis Waitley*

# Happiness is nothing more than good health and a bad memory. *Albert Schweitzer*

There is no greater sorrow than to recall happiness in times of misery. **Dante**

Happiness is secured through virtue;
it is a good attained by man's own will.
**Thomas Aquinas**

It is the chiefest point
of happiness that a
man is willing to be
what he is. *Erasmus*

# Happiness is a by-product of function, purpose, and conflict; those who seek happiness for itself seek victory without war.

*William S. Burroughs*

That man is richest whose pleasures are cheapest.

**Henry David Thoreau**

A mother's happiness is like a beacon, lighting up the future but reflected also on the past in the guise of fond memories.
**Honoré de Balzac**

Happiness is brief. It will not stay.
God batters at its sails. *Euripides*

**The happiness of life is made up of minute fractions – the little, soon forgotten charities of a kiss or a smile, a kind look or heartfelt compliment.**

*Samuel Taylor Coleridge*

# If you want to be happy, live in the present.

Our envy always lasts longer than the happiness of those we envy. *Heraclitus*

When a man has lost all happiness, he's not alive. Call him a breathing corpse.

*Sophocles*

**Happiness always depends on wisdom**

Happiness is a virtue, not its reward.
*Baruch Spinoza*

# The happiness of the bee and the dolphin is to exist. For man it is to know that and to wonder at it.

*Jacques Cousteau*

Let someone know when you're happy, even if it's only yourself.

**Knowledge of what is possible is the beginning of happiness.**

*George Santayana*

# There are as many kinds of beauty as there are habitual ways of seeking happiness.

*Charles Baudelaire*

# Happiness never lays its finger on its pulse. *Adam Smith*

Some pursue happiness, others create it.
*George Sand*

Don't wait around for other people to be happy for you. Any happiness you get you've got to make yourself.
*Alice Walker*

**Happiness is the only good. The time to be happy is now. The place to be happy is here. The way to be happy is to make others so.**
*Robert Green Ingersoll*

The search for happiness is one of the chief sources of unhappiness. *Eric Hoffer*

# A child's smile, a warm summer's day; these are the gifts that make us happiest.

Joy, rather than happiness, is the goal of life, for joy is the emotion which accompanies our fulfilling our natures as human beings. It is based on the experience of one's identity as a being of worth and dignity.

**Rollo May**

It is not true that suffering ennobles the character; happiness does that sometimes, but suffering for the most part, makes men petty and vindictive.

**W. Somerset Maugham**

**Do not speak of your happiness to one less fortunate than yourself.**
*Plutarch*

# Happiness is a how; not a what. A talent, not an object.

*Hermann Hesse*

# Happiness is a choice that requires effort at times. *Aeschylus*

**The greater part of our happiness or misery depends on our dispositions and not our circumstances.**

*Martha Washington*

Happiness is like a butterfly which, when pursued, is always beyond our grasp, but, if you will sit down quietly, may alight upon you.
**Nathaniel Hawthorne**

# Happiness is a thing to be practised, like the violin. *John Lubbock*

**A man's as miserable as he thinks he is.**
*Seneca*

Everyone chases
after happiness,
not noticing that
happiness is right at
their heels.

*Bertolt Brecht*

**Jumping for joy is good exercise.**

**Happiness is a matter of one's most ordinary and everyday mode of consciousness being busy and lively and unconcerned with self.** *Iris Murdoch*

# Try to be happy; but don't try too hard.

When neither their property nor their honour is touched, the majority of men live content.
*Niccolò Machiavelli*

Happiness always looks small when you hold it in your hands, but let it go and you learn at once how big and precious it is.

*Maxim Gorky*

**The happiness of the droplet is to die in the river.** *Al-Ghazali*

Three grand essentials to happiness in this life are something to do, something to love, and something to hope for.
**Joseph Addison**

Gather the crumbs of happiness and they will make you a loaf of contentment.

# What is happiness except the simple harmony between a man and the life he leads? *Albert Camus*

**We act as though comfort and luxury were the chief requirements in life, when all we need to make us really happy is something to be enthusiastic about.** *Charles Kingsley*

Count your blessings rather than your cash; that way, you will be happy.

Even a happy life cannot be without a measure of darkness, and the word 'happy' would lose its meaning if it were not balanced by sadness. *Carl Jung*

# It is an illusion that youth is happy, an illusion of those who have lost it.

*W. Somerset Maugham*

The pursuit of happiness is a most ridiculous phrase; if you pursue happiness, you will never find it. *C.P. Snow*

**The best remedy for those who are afraid, lonely, or unhappy, is to go outside, somewhere where they can be quiet, alone with the heavens, nature, and God. Understand that the right to choose your path is a sacred privilege. Use it. Dwell in possibility.** *Oprah Winfrey*

The best remedy for those who are afraid, lonely or unhappy is to go outside, somewhere where they can be quite alone with the heavens, nature and God. Because only then does one feel that all is as it should be and that God wishes to see people happy, amid the simple beauty of nature.
*Anne Frank*

There is only one happiness in life, to love and be loved. *George Sand*

You may smile because you are happy; or smiling may make you happy.

**What we call happiness in the strictest sense comes from the (preferably sudden) satisfaction of needs which have been dammed up to a high degree.**

*Sigmund Freud*

# Name your blessings, one by one, every day.

**Actions are right in proportion as they tend to promote happiness; wrong as they tend to produce the reverse of happiness. By happiness is intended pleasure and the absence of pain.** *John Stuart Mill*

# What is happiness? The feeling that power increases, that resistance is being overcome.

*Friedrich Nietzsche*

The soul's joy lies in doing.
**Percy Bysshe Shelley**

# Happiness often sneaks through a door you didn't know you'd left open. *John Barrymore*

# Our
# Quest

**The path to happiness lies through travel, sometimes in a literal sense, more often as a spiritual journey. What is our quest, and how do we fulfil it?**

# Travel teaches us how to see.

*African proverb*

No one person can effect great changes. But many people can bring small changes.

You can travel a well-worn path through life, or go off the beaten track. If you do the latter, you may risk getting lost, but you can bet it will be an adventure.

**Try to focus on the present, otherwise you'll miss the good stuff – the here and now!**

You don't have to go anywhere to get somewhere.

A true friend laughs at your jokes when they're not very good, and sympathizes with your troubles when they're not very bad.

# Every path has its puddle.

# The heart that truly loves never forgets.

Don't expect people to be the way you want them to be. Try instead to see them as they are, and to respect their uniqueness.

Don't always run from, or run to. Sometimes, just run.

**Enjoy your own company; that way, you need never feel lonely.**

Be more fully aware of what is all around you – what you can see, hear, touch, and taste.

# Nothing ventured, nothing gained.

Have a kindness day – one day a week, try to perform at least five different acts of kindness for different people.

We have eyes to see the beauty of all that is around us … ears to hear the music of nature … and feet to feel the grass grow …

**Focus on your breathing. Is it light, shallow? Fast, slow? Does it feel different when you slow down and take your time?**

Travel is the frivolous part of a serious life, and the serious part of a frivolous one.

# Kindness is good for you.

Be there for your children – they need your attention, whatever their age.

# Never believe that you have stopped learning.

**Regrets and resentments are a heavy burden to bear. Offload them, and you will walk with a quicker step.**

Fool around. Be silly. Playing isn't just for kids!

**Being kind to strangers helps build a sense of trust and safety in the community around us.**

Dedicate time to your loved ones – being together brings you closer.

Having close personal ties has been shown to have health benefits – slowing mental decline, increasing immunity to disease, and lowering the risk of heart disease.

Give yourself a fixed amount of time to wallow in misery. Then stop!

**Set limits for your children, but also listen to them. Unconditional love combined with clear rules.**

# Know and be known.

If someone new moves in to your area, call on them and make them feel welcome. You might make a new friend...

Don't take your relationships for granted. They need to be nurtured like a garden of flowers.

# Positive emotions nourish us.

Be frivolous from time to time. It's essential!

**Discover what makes you come alive, and bring more joy into your life.**

If you feel blocked and frustrated in life, write down the problems you have. It will clear your head, and help you to move on.

# Spirituality has three stages: discovery, practice, and struggle.

# What do you hold sacred in your life? Whatever it is, nurture it ...

If you feel down, be honest with yourself and think about why. And then move on.

# He who dares, wins.

The path to happiness is a pilgrimage that everyone must make for themselves.

When you can admire, and not desire, you will have found the path to happiness.

**Study the trees: the texture of bark, the sound of leaves, how they move in the wind, birds in the branches, insects buzzing, sunlight through the foliage.**

Make sure you stop to help others
as you travel along your way.

# Go forward, go sideways, go upwards. Just don't go backwards.

Travel will take your mind off your cares, if you are lucky; but sometimes, you can find paradise right where you are.

Life is not a race, and the winner is not always the one who finishes first.

Sometimes, we should admit to being unhappy or needing help. If we are too proud to ask, we may become isolated.

# Observe your thoughts and feelings – but don't get too caught up in worrying about them.

Look up at the sky, see the clouds or the stars. Notice the feeling of air, sun, or wind, on your face…

**Acknowledge the moments when you are sad or disappointed; don't try to brush them aside. Do the same for others, especially children.**

# Happiness is not all about you – it's about sharing with others.

Performing several small kind acts in a day is better than simply trying to be a kind person generally. Variety and spontaneity are the key.

As you walk along, notice how the soles of your feet touch the ground. When your mind begins to wander, bring it back to this simple activity.

**Happiness is a skill we can learn.**

**Do not be overshadowed by the mountains all around you. Instead, take pleasure in the peaceful valley that you find yourself in.**

Don't be afraid to be assertive. People can cope with conflict if they know that it can be resolved peacefully.

# The path to happiness is simple – be kind to others, relax, and be thankful for what you have

The 'helper's high' is the rush of happiness you get from being kind to others.

Love is essential to brain development in the early years of life.

# Travel light – don't carry the weight of the world on your shoulders.

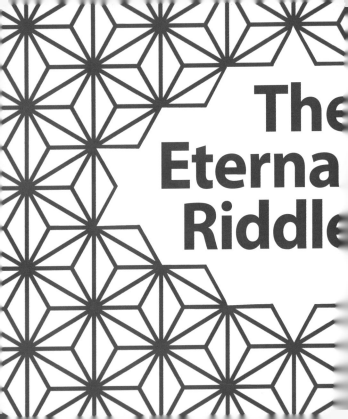

# The Eterna Riddle

A lighthearted look at some of the questions we ask, and the answers we find, in our struggle to solve the eternal mystery of how to be happy.

A person is never happy except at the price of some ignorance.

# Cherish all your happy moments; they make a fine cushion for old age.

**A lifetime of happiness?
No man could bear it.
It would be hell on earth.**

*George Bernard Shaw*

**The memory of happiness makes us sad.**

Happiness is having a large, loving,
close-knit family in another city.
***George Burns***

# Happiness breaks easily, like glass.

Whoever said money doesn't buy happiness didn't know where to shop.

# If only we'd stop trying to be happy we could have a pretty good time.

*Edith Wharton*

Waste not fresh tears over old griefs.

# Nobody really cares if you're miserable, so you might as well be happy.

*Cynthia Nelms*

When ambition ends, happiness begins.

What a wonderful life I've had!
I only wish I'd realized it sooner.
*Colette*

**It's never too late to have a happy childhood.**
*Berkeley Breathed*

# Happiness spring-cleans the heart.

Of all the things you wear, your expression is the most important.

*Janet Lane*

**A truly happy person is one who can enjoy the scenery while on a detour.**

Happiness held is the seed;
happiness shared is the flower.

**The best
vitamin to
be a happy
person is B1.**

The secret of happiness is to find a congenial monotony.

*V.S. Pritchett*

# Real elation is when you feel you could touch a star without standing on tiptoe. *Doug Larson*

# Cheerfulness is what greases the axles of the world. Don't go through life creaking!

*H.W. Byles*

Happiness is not a horse;
you cannot harness it.

# What I'm looking for is a blessing that's not in disguise.

*Kitty O'Neill Collins*

Happiness is the feeling you're feeling when you want to keep feeling it.

# Ask yourself whether you are happy and you cease to be so.

*John Stuart Mill*

# He that travels far knows much. *Persian proverb*

Some people cause happiness wherever they go; others, whenever they go. **Oscar Wilde**

Life is ours to be spent, not saved.
**D.H. Lawrence**

# Happiness does not give, it only lends.

**One should be either sad or joyful. Contentment is a warm sty for eaters and sleepers.** *Eugene O'Neill*

Happiness lies in the secret heart of a lover.

**It is strange what contempt men have for the joys that are offered them freely.**

*Georges Duhamel*

Happiness is a place between too little and too much.

**Eden is that old-fashioned house we dwell in every day Without suspecting our abode until we drive away.**

*Emily Dickinson*

Happiness is the natural flower of duty.

*Phillips Brooks*

To be stupid, selfish, and have good health are three requirements for happiness, though if stupidity is lacking, all is lost. **Gustave Flaubert**

For every minute you are angry, you lose sixty seconds of happiness.

# Without the rain, there would be no rainbow.

Happiness; an agreeable sensation arising from contemplating the misery of another. *Ambrose Bierce*

Cheerfulness is the very flower of health.

# Where you are not – there is happiness.

The world is full of people on a quest for happiness, never knowing that contentment is a place they already know.

He who plants a garden plants happiness.

**Happiness rarely keeps company with an empty stomach.**

# Where there is laughter, there is happiness.

Haggis and a loyal dog are all a man needs for happiness.

*Scottish proverb*

Love is the condition in which another person's happiness is essential to your own.
*Robert Heinlein*

# Obedience is the mother of happiness.

# Happiness is a field you can harvest at every season.

When we pursue happiness,
we flee from contentment.

# Don't worry, be happy.

*Bobby McFerrin*

**Who cleans away every speck of dirt washes away happiness, too.**

# Happiness can grow from a tiny seed of contentment.

We would often be sorry if our wishes were granted. So be careful what you wish for!

# Don't do whatever you like – like whatever you do.

But let there be spaces in your togetherness and let the winds of the heavens dance between you. Love one another but make not a bond of love: let it rather be a moving sea between the shores of your souls. *Khalil Gibran*

Everyone smiles in the same language.

If you wish to be like
someone else, you waste
the person you are.

When you are describing
A shape, or sound, or tint
Don't state the matter plainly
But put it in a hint
And learn to look at all things
With a sort of mental squint.

*Lewis Carroll*